THE SCIENCE OF **SUPERPOWERS**

THE SCIENCE OF
SUPER STRENGTH AND SUPER SPEED

Rani Iyer

Cavendish
Square

New York

Published in 2019 by Cavendish Square Publishing, LLC
243 5th Avenue, Suite 136, New York, NY 10016

Website: cavendishsq.com

This publication represents the opinions and views of the author based on his or her personal experience, knowledge, and research. The information in this book serves as a general guide only. The author and publisher have used their best efforts in preparing this book and disclaim liability rising directly or indirectly from the use and application of this book.

All websites were available and accurate when this book was sent to press.

Library of Congress Cataloging-in-Publication Data

Names: Iyer, Rani, author.
Title: The science of super strength and super speed / Rani Iyer.
Description: First edition. | New York : Cavendish Square, 2019. | Series: The science of superpowers | Audience: Grades 3-6. | Includes bibliographical references and index.
Identifiers: LCCN 2017048760 (print) | LCCN 2017056624 (ebook) | ISBN 9781502637956 (ebook) | ISBN 9781502637932 (library bound) | ISBN 9781502637949 (pbk.)
Subjects: LCSH: Science--Miscellanea--Juvenile literature. | Superheroes--Miscellanea--Juvenile literature. | Technological innovations--Juvenile literature.
Classification: LCC Q175.2 (ebook) | LCC Q175.2 .I94 2019 (print) | DDC 502--dc23
LC record available at https://lccn.loc.gov/2017048760

Editorial Director: David McNamara
Editor: Kristen Susienka
Copy Editor: Rebecca Rohan
Associate Art Director: Amy Greenan
Designer: Joe Parenteau
Production Coordinator: Karol Szymczuk
Photo Research: J8 Media

Printed in the United States of America

CONTENTS

CHAPTER 1

SUPERHEROES IN HISTORY

Humans have enjoyed stories of superpowers since the first civilizations formed. The lives and lessons learned from heroes in legends of the past teach us. They help our imaginations grow. They also have us asking: Could these superpowers ever be real? Today, there are some humans and animals that have certain "superpowers." Two such "powers" are super

Opposite: Rock climbing is a dangerous sport. Expert rock climbers have to be very strong to pull themselves onto rocks.

strength and super speed. But what makes such "powers" possible? And how did these abilities influence ancient stories?

ANCIENT SUPERHEROES

Ancient carvings, paintings, and writings show great **deeds** of heroic men and women. There are many **myths**, songs, and legends about heroes. Heroes' bravery is celebrated in every culture. For the ancient people, heroes were important parts of their lives. They gave people hope that ordinary people could do extraordinary things. The superheroes had exciting adventures in faraway places. The stories were entertaining. Some of them described the physical and mental strength of the heroes.

Some of the most well-known examples of ancient heroes

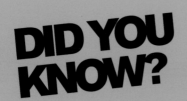

DID YOU KNOW?

One of the strongest men ever recorded in history was Louis Cyr, a Canadian who lived in the late 1800s and early 1900s. He could lift a horse over his head!

The Romans told exciting stories about heroes. Some heroes even raced each other with chariots. This mosaic shows a chariot race in Rome.

come from Egyptian, Greek, and Roman cultures. The ancient Egyptians, Greeks, and Romans believed in many gods. Some of these gods had children with humans. These children had superpowers. A popular story from Greek and Roman mythology is the tale of Heracles (also called Hercules). Heracles was a strong human. He could wrestle monsters and lift large rocks.

People who listened to his story wanted to be like Heracles. Other examples of legends with super strength were the Titans. Titans were the children of gods too. An Egyptian god named Apis had super strength also. Super fast heroes existed too. One example was Hermes, a messenger god in Greek mythology. His shoes had wings that made him fly with great speed.

Heracles performed legendary deeds, such as killing monsters. Here he is shown wrestling a boar.

TRAITS OF HEROES

Many heroes used their superpowers to help others. Some heroes had tools or special weapons, which gave them super strength. Other heroes had special shoes or helmets that made them super fast.

Heroes were always ready to go on their next quest. They needed very little preparation. The enemies usually had more powers than the heroes. The heroes used a combination of intelligence and strength to win. They could smash through obstacles using their strength. They used their intelligence to decide what was best for the situation.

HEROES IN LEGENDS, MYTHS, AND FOLKLORE

Many heroes in legends moved freely between worlds inhabited by gods and people. Heroes performed amazing deeds, such as holding up the sky, shrinking in size, or lifting mountains. They killed monstrous birds and animals. Many performed feats that required them to fly or perform seemingly impossible tasks quickly. Sometimes heroes also performed bad deeds to help their friends.

Atalanta: A Rare Hero

Ancient Greek mythology has many heroes. Most of them were men. Atalanta, however, was a female Greek hero. She had the powers of both super strength and super speed. She was born a princess. However, her father wanted a son. He left her on a mountaintop to die. After being saved by bears, Atalanta spent her life with them. She learned to hunt like a bear. One popular story about Atalanta involves her killing a boar sent by the goddess Artemis to destroy a kingdom. She hunted and killed the boar, saving the kingdom. Atalanta was given the boar's **hide** as a prize.

Soon after the hunt, Atalanta was discovered by her father. He took her home. He wanted her to marry. Atalanta agreed to marry anyone who beat her in a footrace. Hippomenes, one of the heroes of the boar hunt, knew he could not outrun Atalanta. To distract her, he got three golden apples from the goddess Aphrodite. Every time Hippomenes dropped the apples in the race, Atalanta helped pick them up. This way, Hippomenes made sure Atalanta lost the race. The two married and had a son. Atalanta is an example of a clever and courageous hero. She has appeared in paintings and other artwork.

This painting shows Hippomenes (*left*) distracting Atalanta (*right*) during their race.

This sculpture shows the Greek god Hermes. He had winged shoes and a winged helmet.

The Science of Super Strength and Super Speed

Super strong and super fast heroes have been a part of cultures all around the world. They came from all walks of life. Heracles, for example, was an athlete. Cadmus brought the alphabet to Greece. Daedalus was an inventor and craftsman. Some were kings. Others were shepherds. Many of them were warriors. Heroes were humans, gods, or **demigods**.

The super strong heroes had a different type of body. They were normally muscular. The muscles could bear nonstop work. Their bones were strong. They did not break easily. They could act quickly due to their super speed. They were immune to some weapons.

History and folklore are full of well-known stories about people with super strength and super speed. Exactly how super strength and super speed work involves many parts of the body working together.

CHAPTER 2

HOW IS IT POSSIBLE?

Today, science can explain a lot of what happens to a body when it exercises. Some heroes had to exercise to keep up their super strength and super speed. Today, if someone is very strong or very fast, they might have different **genes** that help them become that way. They also might have to spend a long time training their body to do different exercises. Training could take

Opposite: Champion weightlifters have strong muscles. They can lift objects that weigh twice their own body weight.

A disease called myostatin-related muscular hypertrophy gives some people very large muscles. Only two human beings have been discovered to have it. These people have up to twice the amount of muscle a typical human has.

months or years. So, how are super strength or super speed possible today?

Muscles are the key to super strength and super speed. Scientists know this from studying both humans and animals. Humans and animals have many muscles that work in different ways to create super strength or super speed. It is important to strengthen your muscles if you want to be able to lift heavy objects or run very fast.

There are certain **proteins** in your body that help muscles grow. Myostatin is one of them. Myostatin controls how big your muscles can be. Another protein called Activin A stops super muscle growth. Myostatin and Activin A keep the size and number of muscle cells under control. This means when both proteins are present, your muscles can grow, but not too big.

Super-fast runners have strong leg muscles. These women are competing in the Olympics in 2016.

Leg muscles help you become super fast. If you work hard and do exercises, you can become a faster runner or walker. Some exercises that can strengthen your leg muscles include swimming, bicycling, and walking. However, your legs aren't the only things that can help you run or walk fast. You also have to eat healthy food, have the right **posture**, understand how to breathe while exercising, and have a strong middle, called a core.

THE POWER OF SUPER SPEED

To better understand why some people can run super fast, scientists study athletes and animals. Athletes spend many hours each day training their muscles. Animals also have certain muscles and features that help them run fast.

Humans can't run too fast, but there are some people who are able to run at faster-than-normal

Usain Bolt races to the finish line in 2015. Notice the length of his stride.

speeds. For example, the fastest runner ever recorded is Usain Bolt. He ran a 100-meter (109-yard) race in 9.58 seconds. If he ran at that pace for a whole mile, he would finish in 2.5 minutes!

Usain Bolt and other fast runners like him can run quickly because of how their bodies are built. They have strong muscles and small bodies. Most runners in the Olympics are very thin. That helps them move quicker because there is less weight for them to carry as they run.

Fast animals are also thinner. Cheetahs are the fastest land animals on Earth. They can run

The cheetah, the fastest land animal, is built to run.

at 75 miles per hour (121 kilometers per hour). Their tails also help them balance and change directions when they run. This lets cheetahs chase their **prey**.

Some animals can react to situations very quickly. For example, some reptiles have super fast tongues they use to catch their prey. Humans can also become super fast if they are scared or in a dangerous situation. Something called **adrenaline** gives humans a boost of energy and helps them do superhuman things, like lift cars off injured people or run fast from a dangerous fire.

GENES AND METABOLISM

Sometimes, genes your parents give you help you grow bigger muscles or become a faster runner or walker. There are also some genes that let you grow very small muscles or very large muscles. You get more strength when you have more muscles. Remember that Myostatin controls the size and number of your muscle cells. When Myostatin is removed, muscle size and strength improves.

Metabolism is also important to helping your body grow, process food, and produce energy. Everyone has a certain rate of metabolism. If you

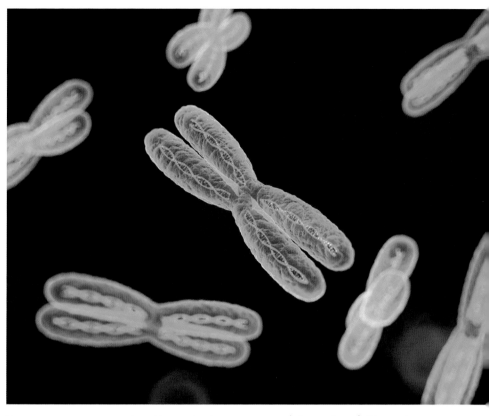

Your genes are passed on through chromosomes (shown here). They play an important role in your metabolism.

eat a lot and have a high metabolism, you may not gain much weight. As your body gets older, though, your metabolism slows down. That can make you gain more weight and slow you down. Doing exercises like lifting weights and running or walking can increase your metabolism and help you burn fat. They can also help you become stronger and faster.

Extra Strength via Exoskeleton Suit

This man demonstrates an exoskeleton suit at TechCrunch Sessions: Robotics, a single-day event about technologies, in July 2017.

Soldiers in the battlefield carry heavy equipment. A soldier's backpack weighs about 150 to 170 pounds (68 to 77 kilograms). When soldiers have to lift heavy things, carry them, drop them off, or trek long distances, it causes muscle strain.

To help soldiers, the military has built an **exoskeleton** suit. It gives

GENE TECHNOLOGIES

Today, scientists are using gene technology to make stronger muscles. Using gene technology, scientists have changed the muscle size and muscle strength of rats and monkeys. One popular gene-changing invention is CRISPR. It allows genes to be changed in some animals and insects to help stop the spread of human diseases. For example, malaria is a common disease in soldiers extra strength. By wearing this suit, soldiers can easily lift up to 200 pounds (90.71 kg)! One of the best parts about the exoskeleton is that soldiers don't notice the heavy weight. It feels like the backpack is only 10 pounds (4.53 kilograms)!

The exoskeleton is light and flexible. However, it does not cover the whole body. It covers only the hands and legs. It is powered by **high-pressure hydraulics**. A high-pressure hydraulics system gives the exoskeleton its strength and helps it lift heavy objects. The suit needs to be refilled by fuel every eight hours. It is not yet ready to go on the battlefield with the soldiers. However, scientists hope it will one day help soldiers there too. A similar concept is also being developed for everyday people to use.

tropical countries. It affects humans. Mosquitoes are known for bringing malaria to humans through mosquito bites. Using CRISPR, scientists have been able to change the genes of mosquitoes so that they cannot reproduce and spread the disease further. Even though this idea works in laboratories, it does not mean it will work in the wild. Still, it is hoped that it can one day eliminate certain deadly diseases from the world.

CHAPTER 3

A REAL POWER FOR SOME

In the animal world, there are many examples of super strong and super fast creatures. Some of these animals or insects look small and weak, but they have strong bodies that let them lift seemingly impossible objects or run fast. Scientists judge a creature's strength using **proportional strength**. They study how the animal or insect's body looks and how much

Opposite: Elephants are strong. They can easily lift heavy trees.

weight they can lift. An elephant, for example, can easily lift about 200 pounds (90.71 kg) with its trunk. This is about one-quarter its own weight. A rhinoceros beetle, on the other hand, can grow up to 8 inches (about 20 centimeters) long and weighs about 3 ounces (85 grams). The male beetle can lift a giant dung ball and carry it. For a human being to match this effort, they would need to lift 180,000 pounds (81,647 kg). That weighs about the same as seven school buses!

DID YOU KNOW?

Tardigrades, the hardiest creatures on the planet, are barely a millimeter in size. These water-dwelling microanimals survived the ride to outer space and back.

SUPER FAST ANIMALS

The fastest animal is the peregrine falcon. It can dive through the air at 250 miles per hour (402 kmh). However, other animals have fast speeds too. The fastest sprint ever recorded on camera happened in 2011. A cheetah sprinted 100 meters (109 yards) in 5.95 seconds. That is

A peregrine falcon can dive faster than a cheetah can sprint!

four seconds faster than Usain Bolt! In the water, the black marlin is the fastest sea animal. It can reach speeds of 80 miles per hour (129 kmh).

Animals with super speed have similar characteristics. This is called a "body plan." They have sleek, slender, and light bodies. The cheetah can speed up from 0 to 40 miles per hour (0 to 64 kmh) in a few strides. It weighs just under 125 pounds (57 kg). With a small head, flattened rib cage and thin legs, a cheetah easily pushes

Speedy Mice

Scientists and researchers conduct experiments on animals that give them super strength or super speed. One example comes from Switzerland. In 2011, scientists there used gene treatment to turn normal mice into "speedy" mice.

To do this, the scientists "switched off" a

Mice have been used in experiments testing super speed.

gene in muscle cells but kept the **mitochondria** working. Mitochondria are the brains of a cell. The results amazed scientists. The mice that received gene treatment grew muscles. They raced twice as fast as normal mice. They could also run twenty minutes longer than normal mice. Unlike humans, who need more food to energize them, the "speedy" mice did not eat more than normal mice.

This had researchers wondering if mitochondria could be switched off in human cells to produce speedy humans. Scientists are studying this further, but there may be dangers in testing this and using this treatment on humans.

through the air. Cheetahs have larger eyes to get a wide-angle view of their surroundings. Their spines are extra flexible and act as a spring for their back legs. A cheetah's large tail acts as a rudder and balances the cheetah when it sprints. The entire body of a cheetah is built for speed.

ANTS

Although they are small, ants have super strength. Ant colonies are actually complex societies. Each ant in the colony takes on a different role and belongs to a different caste, or class. A typical ant colony has a queen, worker ants (usually female), and male ants, called drones. Ants can lift objects and carry them long distances. Many times these objects are much heavier than the ants. In fact, some ants can carry between 350 to 1,000 times their body weight for long distances. An example is leafcutter ants. They cut down leaves and can carry them 100 feet (30 meters) to their colonies. The American field ant's neck can also withstand pressure of 5,000 times its body weight.

Some ants show super strength another way. Some worker ants act as the colony's soldiers. These soldiers guard the group. One special group, mostly found in ants belonging to the species *Pheidole*, is the giant-headed "super soldiers." They are "super" because they have enormous heads. They use their oversized heads to push back any invaders.

In 2012, scientists discovered that other ant species could create super soldiers too. That is because super soldiers are mutants. That means they have body parts or traits that are different from the rest of their species. Mutations are created when an organism's genes change unexpectedly as the animal develops. Mutations can appear in any species of plant or animal. A genetic mutation thousands of years ago caused a person to have the first pair of blue eyes.

Scientists have created these super ants in laboratories as well. In the wild, all ants receive special diets that prepare them for their life and role in the colony. The diets support certain types of hormonal development. The queen, for example, receives a special diet. The **hormones** in the diet control the size of the insects as they grow. A researcher named Dr. Ehab Abouheif, from Montreal, Canada, used special hormones to create "super soldier" ants in a species that did not have the mutation in their genes. Can this happen in humans too?

An anthill's superheroes

Within an ant colony, individuals develop into different forms with different roles, and a few may become extra-large.

Genes, hormones and diet influence shapes of castes

Worker digs tunnels, moves food and waste, cares for larvae

Soldier repels predators and raids by other colonies

Queen has wings, usually the only ant that lays eggs

Worker

Super soldier has giant head and large, powerful body

Super soldier can block anthill tunnels with its head and jaws

Pheidole ants (southwest U.S. and Mexico)

Why do they occur?

Super soldiers occur naturally in some ant species

Some ants react to stress by expanding in size

© 2012 MCT
Source: R. Rajakumar of McGill University, Science
Graphic: Helen Lee McComas

This illustration shows different ants in an ant colony and how super-soldier ants are created.

Super strong women and men can lift incredibly heavy objects. This woman is lifting a giant tire.

THE STRONGEST HUMANS

Today, there are competitions every year to see who is the strongest person on Earth. According to the Strongman and Strongwoman Competitions of 2017, the strongest man was Eddie Hall from the United Kingdom, and the strongest woman was Leslie Hofheins from the United States.

Men and women who join these competitions lift, pull, and carry incredibly heavy objects. Some people pull cars, tractors, fire trucks, or semi-trucks to win an event.

Super strong people have large muscles. They lift weights every day. Sometimes they lift weights more than once a day. It is possible to become super strong on your own. You must have the right equipment and know what you are doing. Often, people who want to become super strong have help from personal trainers.

CHAPTER 4

APPLYING THE POWER

The science of super strength and super speed tells us many things. We know how animals with super strength function. We know how humans can become super strong through exercising. We know that some genes give us super strength or super speed. We know the limitations of the human body. Today, people are using this knowledge to design new technology that

Opposite: With the help of jet packs, people can speed into the air and "fly" short distances.

makes even stronger and faster humans possible. Companies like Lockheed Martin, the Defense Advanced Research Projects Agency (DARPA), and Daewoo are working hard to produce innovative and impressive inventions. Their technology will help us to overcome the limits of the human body. In recent years, new discoveries and technologies have become available for experiencing super strength and speed. Many of these technologies are still under development. However, some are available for everyone to use.

SUPER SPEED MACHINES AND TESTS

When you think of a jet pack, you might think of flying. However, jet packs are also being used today to help people gain super speed. DARPA, an organization belonging to the US military, has developed a special kind of jet pack. It keeps people on the ground but helps them run faster. In 2014, they tested their jet pack. It helped soldiers run four-minute miles without much effort, even though the jet pack weighed 11.2 pounds (5 kg).

Inventors and sports enthusiasts are also trying to master the ability to run a marathon in under two hours. A marathon is a long-distance race. The history of the marathon goes back to the ancient Olympics. The modern marathon is a road race 26.2 miles (42.2 km) long. The current world record time for a marathon is two hours, two minutes, and fifty-seven seconds. Dennis Kimetto, a runner from Kenya, set that record in 2014. Since then, many scientists and experts have predicted that it will be possible to run a marathon in under two hours. This is called a sub-two-hour marathon.

Running a marathon is very difficult for many people. It puts a lot of strain on the body. To run a marathon in under two hours would take lots of training. Some experts think that running barefoot will help runners reach sub-two-hour speeds. Others think

DID YOU KNOW?

In 2017, English inventor Richard M. Browning built his own jet pack. It is called the Daedalus. It is named after the Greek myth of Icarus. The story of Icarus tells of a boy who escapes a prison with his father, Daedalus, using wings made of feathers and wax. However, Icarus flies too close to the sun, his wings melt, and he dies. The jet pack Browning created can carry him across the ground in any direction. However, it can't go higher than a few meters off the ground.

that reaching the sub-two-hour speed will require special equipment to prepare runners for the race.

In 2014, the athletic company Nike trained three runners to run a sub-two-hour marathon. They spent three years preparing the runners. People invented new shoes for the runners. They tested them on treadmills. Then, in May 2017, the runners raced an unofficial marathon in Italy. One of the runners, Eliud Kipchoge, finished in two hours and twenty-three seconds. The goal of the race was to show that a sub-two-hour marathon

Eliud Kipchoge finishes his attempt at a sub-two-hour marathon in May 2017. He came close when he clocked two hours twenty-three seconds.

was possible. While he didn't finish in under two hours, he was very close. Scientists think that humans will be able to complete a sub-two-hour marathon between the years 2025 and late 2030. They are still inventing new ways to help runners reach faster times.

TECHNOLOGIES AND SUPER STRENGTH

New technologies like exoskeletons are helping workers other than soldiers too. In 2014, the Daewoo Shipbuilding and Marine Engineering Company introduced an exoskeleton to its shipyard workers in South Korea.

Shipyards are places of extreme human labor. The tools are heavy. Workers often have to work in tight corners with the heavy tools. How long can you hold a 30-pound (13.60 kg) tool when it is extended away from your body? Most adults can hold it for about three minutes. Using heavy tools causes people to get tired and can injure muscles. Like the ones being developed for soldiers, the exoskeletons Daewoo designed were made to help lift objects. Workers wore an unpowered, lightweight exoskeleton to do their job. The exoskeleton gave the power of super strength to the workers. They could lift heavy tools such as

Super Speed: Breaking the Sound Barrier

Speed is not only measured on Earth. On October 14, 2012, it was also measured in space. That year, a project called Red Bull Stratos wanted to test the limits of the speed of sound. They decided to do this by sending a speed skydiver into space. He would fall to Earth and try to break the sound barrier. Speed skydiving can only be performed by people trained for it. Speed skydivers test the limits of speed by going high up into the atmosphere and falling to Earth. At high altitudes, the **force** of gravity is intense. Many divers lose consciousness and spin out of control. Only expert skydivers can complete such a mission.

An Austrian pilot named Felix Baumgartner volunteered to go into space. He was an experienced speed skydiver. First, he was sent into the atmosphere in a special balloon. Then, he jumped out of it from 128,100 feet (39,045 m)

grinders, riveters, or sandblasters without strain. The workers were able to hold heavy tools for twenty minutes. The exoskeleton also reduced tiredness and strain-related injuries.

Australian space diver Felix Baumgartner prepares to dive down to Earth in 2012.

up. This daring dive was streamed live. Millions of people around the world watched it on TV or on their computers. Thirty-four seconds into the jump, Baumgartner reached 833.6 miles per hour (1,342 kmh). This speed is equivalent to 1.25 times the speed of sound. The fall lasted four minutes and twenty seconds. By the end of it, Felix Baumgartner had become the first person to break the sound barrier.

Prosthetic inventions are becoming more common too. In 2013, students at the University of Pennsylvania designed a super strong arm called the Titan Arm. This upper-body exoskeleton strapped on to the wearer's right arm. It was battery powered, made of steel, and designed with the wearer's comfort in mind. It was also rumored to give the wearer the strength of Heracles. In reality, it could lift 40 pounds (18 kg). The designers intended for it to be used in physical therapy patients. For their efforts, the designers won the 2013 James Dyson Award, a prize given to new student innovators and their inventions.

Elizabeth Beattie Hunter, who helped develop the Titan Arm, demonstrates it in 2015.

Inventors like those working at Daewoo and in engineering schools have developed exciting new technologies. Every year, science competitions and fairs encourage more inventors to develop new creations. It will be exciting to see how super strength technologies develop in the future.

GLOSSARY

ADRENALINE A system in the body that gives you more energy in a dangerous or frightening situation.

DEED A job that a hero does.

DEMIGOD A character that is half human, half god.

EXOSKELETON A suit people wear that helps them lift heavy objects.

FORCE An outside pressure on the body.

GENE A part of DNA that contains genetic information.

HIDE The fur or skin of an animal.

HIGH-PRESSURE HYDRAULICS A motor that converts mechanical energy into fluid energy using liquid such as mineral oil or water.

HORMONE A part of the body that helps you grow from a child into an adult.

METABOLISM A part of the body that helps give you energy and burn fat.

MITOCHONDRIA A part of the cell that provides energy for cells to work.

MYTH A story from an ancient culture.

POSTURE The way a person stands or sits. When exercising, posture is how a person looks.

PREY Animals hunted by other animals.

PROPORTIONAL STRENGTH How strong an animal is based on its body size.

PROSTHETIC An arm or leg that is made of metal or another material.

PROTEIN Hundreds or thousands of small molecules called amino acids join in a long chain to form a complex molecule called protein. Proteins perform many important body functions.

TROPICAL COUNTRIES Nations that lie above and below the equator.

FIND OUT MORE

BOOKS

Berne, Emma Carlson. *Dung Beetles: Stronger Than Ten Men*. New York: PowerKids Press, 2013.

Brown, Jordan. *Unmasking the Science of Superpowers!* New York: Simon Spotlight, 2016.

Hernandez, Christopher. *Animal Superpowers*. New York: Scholastic, 2012.

Jenkins, Steve. *Speediest! 19 Very Fast Animals*. Extreme Animals. New York: Houghton Mifflin Harcourt Books for Young Readers, 2018.

WEBSITES

Conservation Institute: 10 Fastest Animals on Earth

http://www.conservationinstitute.org/10-fastest-animals-on-earth

Visit this website to learn more about the ten fastest animals on the planet.

Eight Superpowers Brought to You By Technology

http://www.popularmechanics.com/technology/g1258/8-superpowers-brought-to-you-by-technology

This website lists eight superpowers that are becoming real thanks to technology.

Red Bull Stratos

http://www.redbullstratos.com

This website explains the story of Felix Baumgartner's fall to Earth.

INDEX

Page numbers in **boldface** are illustrations. Entries in **boldface** are glossary terms.

ABOUT THE AUTHOR

Rani Iyer loves to write about science, nature, culture, human-nature interactions, and natural ecosystems. The author of twelve books and more than one hundred articles, she has doctoral degrees in language, literacy, technology, and ecology. To learn more about her, visit http://www.raniyer.com.